I, Claudia

I, Claudia

Kristen Thomson

Playwrights Canada Press
Toronto • Canada

Playwrights Canada Press
202-269 Richmond St. W.
Toronto, ON M5V 1X1
416.703.0013 • info@playwrightscanada.com • www.playwrightscanada.com

For professional or amateur production rights, please contact:
LeFeaver Talent Management
785 Carlaw Ave., Toronto, ON M4K 3L1
lefeavertalent@canadafilm.com

We acknowledge the financial support of the Canada Council for the Arts, the Ontario Arts
Council, the Ontario Media Development Corporation, and the Government of Canada through
the Canada Book Fund for our publishing activities.

Cover photo of Kristen Thomson as Claudia by Guntar Kravis
Production editor / Cover design by JLArt

Library and Archives Canada Cataloguing in Publication

Thomson, Kristen
I, Claudia / Kristen Thomson.

A play.
ISBN 978-0-88754-674-7

I. Title.

PS8589.H45787I2 2003   C812'.6   C2003-901054-6
PR9199.4T77I2 2003

First edition: May 2003
Sixth printing: November 2012
Printed and bound in Canada by Marquis Book Printing, Montreal

For my mother, Lucinda Williams (née Wiley).

INTRODUCTION

While I hope that the text of *I, Claudia* can stand alone without an introduction, the truth is that the way the play was created has much to do with what you read on the page.

The first thing to know is that I approached writing *I, Claudia* from what I do as an actor. I used improvisation to create the characters, to generate all of the text, and it was only after months of improvisation that the guiding logic for the play itself emerged. You'll see that there is little by way of narrative in the play. Most of the actual stage action is in what the characters do to the audience as they speak their monologues. The connective tissue of the play isn't so much in its narrative movement as in the way that the characters speak across themes, share needs, and collectively build trust and momentum with the audience that allows the whole of the play to be formed.

Masks were the central metaphor and tool for the creation of *I, Claudia*. I improvised with masks to develop the script and eventually to perform the play. The four masks I used were from a larger set of twenty-six that have been used internationally to teach generations of acting students about character development and improvisation. They were designed by Anglo-Algerian stage designer Abdel Kader Farrah. Luckily, I don't have to describe the masks. You can look at the production photos in this publication. What is more difficult, however, is to describe how the masks work.

As taught by their most renowned instructor, Pierre Lefevre, the pedagogy was as follows: A student would choose a mask and in front of a mirror would begin to get an impression of how the mask fit his/her particular physiognomy. The student would then begin to physically and vocally adjust to the mask, which often included adding costume pieces that supported the emerging character. M. Lefevre would create imagined circumstances for the characters to experience. And then slowly, slowly, the student would begin to answer questions posed to them by M. Lefevre. He would often remind us not to try to "wow" the class, but to allow the character to speak from the physicality we had found. Often, when the student was beginning to honestly inhabit a character, the answers given were utterly surprising and original, even for the student speaking. By using the voice and body to create character, normal psychological routes were circumvented, and something edgy and impulsive took over.

So, there I was working with four different masks to create this play, and using the techniques taught to me by M. Lefevre. It is no wonder that the theme of transformation runs under the play, and moments of decisive change define the lives of the characters. I literally had to transform myself to inhabit each character, and that became a controlling metaphor for the play. I improvised in front of a mirror for hours and needed one on stage with me to change from character to character. This is why Drachman's final story ends with the powerful necessity that the little girl see herself reflected. In these ways, working with the masks informed the pre-occupations of the play.

Also, essential to working with the masks is listening to what the characters say. Anything that doesn't come from the masks feels false. I incorporated this fact into the writing process by tape recording all of my improvisations and then transcribing it all word for word, believing that every "um", "like", misused or repeated word was essential. In this way, the voice of each character was allowed to emerge immediate, unmitigated, and idiosyncratic. Then, combing through the transcriptions, I tried to uncover the guiding logic of a larger piece.

In this way, the logic of *I, Claudia* isn't immediately evident. It lies somewhere below the surface in the theatricality of the characters and the depth of their need for the audience.

ACKNOWLEDGEMENTS

I would like to thank the following individuals for their significant contributions to the writing and development of *I, Claudia*: Chris Abraham, my dramaturge, director and friend, who is in every word of the play; Leah Cherniak for guiding me through to the first draft; and especially Urjo Kareda for loving Claudia and accepting full custody. I remember Urjo in my heart, for his encouragement, so freely given.

And thanks to the following friends and colleagues: Perry Schneiderman, Aime Vincent, Andy McKim, Martha Ross and Theatre Columbus, Sarah Polley, Nancy LeFeaver, Andy Massingham, Michelle Smith, Peter Wylde, Paul Lampert, Mark Christman, Jordan Pettle, Steven Souter, Ruth Madoc-Jones, Anton Piatagorsky, Ava Roth, Ted Dykstra, Waneta Storms, Martha Burns, and Arts Toronto 2000 Protégé Honours Program.

Love and thanks to Liisa Repo-Martell, Anke Allspach, Shoshana Pollack, Shirley Russ, Bob Williams, Harvey McKinnon, Marcia Thomson, Todd Thomson, and John Thomson, ALL for your endless nurturing and support. And Hussain Amarshi, your understanding makes my life and my work better.

I, Claudia was first produced by Tarragon Theatre, Toronto, Ontario in April, 2001 with the following company:

DRACHMAN,
CLAUDIA,
DOUGLAS &
LESLIE   Kristen Thomson

Directed by Chris Abraham
Stage Managed by Shauna Janssen
Set & Costume Design by Julie Fox
Lighting Design by Rebecca Picherack
Sound Editor: John Gzowski

—— • —— • ——

Portions of *I, Claudia* were introduced in Theatre Columbus' Mayhem showcase and then subsequently expanded through Tarragon Spring Arts Fairs in 1999 and 2000. The play then moved to several developmental workshops at Tarragon.

CHARACTERS

DRACHMAN
CLAUDIA
DOUGLAS
LESLIE

I, Claudia

A red curtain hangs across the space. DRACHMAN enters, pulls back the curtain, revealing the boiler room of an elementary school and in a magical way, reveals a series of placards: "Drachman Presents"; "I, Claudia"; "Starring Claudia"; "And Others". Then DRACHMAN pretends to look for a fifth placard which he can't find, swears in his native language and addresses the audience.

Drachman

Frescia!

Lady and Gentlemen, please to apologize. I was finding a missing placard – and that was a real disgrace because that was my favourite placard to say welcome to each person that was coming here. So now I must to say on behalf of that placard such a welcome to each person really from my heart, such a welcome. Welcome to each person.

As he goes to leave, DRACHMAN pretends to be surprised to find a top hat.

What the hell is this?

He examines it. There is a flash of fire and DRACHMAN magically produces a butterfly from the top hat. The performer then transforms to become CLAUDIA.

Claudia

Ever stare at yourself so hard that your eyes practically start bleeding? I do.

I invited some girls over to my house to work on our science fair topic. Ya, well, most of them didn't want to come. I don't know. I don't live in the same neighbourhood as them anymore so they said it was too far on the subway to get to my house. But I don't think that's true 'cause it only takes me twenty minutes to get home. So I think they might be lying. I don't know maybe their parents are stunned and don't let them go on the subway right, so maybe that's possible. Some parents are very over-protective of their children. And then others, then some others educate their children to be street smart. And I'm street smart. Yeah. I went to a workshop one weekend with my mother. Well she thought it would be a good idea because now I have to take the subway from my house *and* from my house at my dad's. Some people would say that downtown Toronto is not very safe. But I would not say that at all, right. I would not say that at all. What I think is if you are someplace where there's nobody there then that's not safe right because there's nobody else to kind of protect you or to see, or to see if you might be in trouble. So that's what I say is not safe. If nobody is there to watch you. Right? So, safety is a very big concern for me. Yeah. Yes, it's a very big concern for me for very sickening reasons because you know, there are vulnerable people in this society, and I am one of them. Like if I lived on a farm, if I was like a farm girl, then maybe it wouldn't be so scary just to be alive. Except I might be afraid of getting my hand severed off by a machine. But I live in a very major urban centre and women and children... which is not to say that, not to say, I mean, I know that there are also racist crimes and there are kinds of crimes against people because of their sexuality and there are also crimes against people like if they are poor. Terrible things happen to poor people. I already know that. I already know that. And

Kristen Thomson as CLAUDIA.

Photograph by Guntar Kravis.

I know, I know that I am not poor. Like financially, I'm not very poor at all. Except I'm an only child so I am sibling poor. So, I don't have enough siblings. But I have goldfish. Romeo and Juliet. Two fish, they're really nice and they... I think Romeo might be pregnant. Yeah! Because I got them mixed up. I think that Romeo is a girl and Juliet is a boy! Yeah! I know! But it's hi-larious but it's true. Life is like that sometimes, isn't it? Life is sometimes... sometimes life is so true, it's hi-larious! Don't you find that? So anyway, I think they might be having children, like guppies. Um, is that what you call baby fish? Guppies? And I tell you, that's very satisfying for me. Yeah. And also I want a hamster for my room at my dad's. So cute. Well because in science class we're dissecting frogs, right, so, I don't want a frog because I've already seen one dead. But, but anyways I want a hamster and some gerbils. Something just like, I don't know, just to like enrich my life so I had like a wilderness in both my bedrooms. Like wildlife. Like a eco-system of two apartments and I would be like the migrating bird with two nests, but not like north and south. More like messy and clean. Yeah! My room at my mom's, which is my house, is the messy room. Well, it was the messy room. But my mom said I had to clean it 'cause it was a pigsty with my clothes for carpeting, plus, she said she was going to go through everything with a fine-tooth comb because – now I'm totally embarrassed.

Because I'm going through puberty. Oh my God, I don't even want to talk about it, it's disgusting! Yeah, like oh, oh "you're going through puberty" and everybody thinks they can say things like about if you need a bra or something. It's so embarrassing! It's so disgustingly embarrassing! And you can't even say anything, you can't even say, you can't even say, "STOP IT! STOP IT! STOP IT! STOP TEASING ME!" Right? 'Cause everybody thinks it's so funny and everybody all the grown ups think because they went through it they can just torment you! But they can't. It's totally disgusting and unfair!

As she talks, CLAUDIA gets a snack from her lunch box. She takes out a single man's sock with something in it. She takes a juice box from the sock, sips as she continues to speak, and just tosses the box away carelessly whenever she's finished with it. CLAUDIA should drink as many juice boxes as she wishes throughout the show.

So anyway, because I'm growing, she said she wanted to take a bunch of my stuff that doesn't fit me anymore to the Goodwill and so she said – I had to go through all my stuff, get rid of everything I didn't want anymore and then she said she was gonna go through it all with a fine-tooth comb. My own *Private!* My own *Private* Sanctuary or Domain! She was gonna go through it with a *Fine-Tooth Comb*, that's what she said, you know, exact words, *Fine-Tooth Comb!*

Well, I had some very private objects in my room that isn't stuff I want to give away and isn't stuff that my mom is allowed to comb through. Like, there were things hidden underneath my bed. Like Evidence and secret objects, and personal musings. Like, essentially the whole stock of my private emotional life which I so can't let my mom see and I so can't put it at my dad's because a lot of it is stuff that I... well, um... I kind of... took... or – as the police would say, stole from his apartment. So I can't really put it there 'cause I only get to see him once a week, so he can't think that I'm, like, his criminal daughter who steals from him.

So I brought it all to the school, down here in the basement, in the boiler room, where nobody goes, except me. Weird and mysterious, eh? Oh, and except the janitor, but he doesn't even wreck it for me, he just leaves me alone. So now this is where I hide my stuff. Men's socks go in here.

She jams the sock into an electric box which is already crammed with socks, and from various hiding spots she produces other objects.

DIARY. Sex book. This very terrible coffee mug. Baggy full of hair. Bunch of other stuff. And, on Tuesday mornings, which is the worst day of my entire life, I even come down here to hide my face.

CLAUDIA changes into DRACHMAN. She may begin speaking before the change is fully complete.

Drachman

I am finding that girl down here every Tuesday morning. She is very, I'm going to tell you, she is *mitchka* is what we say. She is too young to think on it but hiding this sock in the electric box could 'cause a very danger. So I am watch always to keep a safety...

He opens the electric box to show how he has sectioned off the interior.

So, you see, I was make this barrier here. And so the sock is separated from the electrical wire, and so. But still, I am watching for her... because she is *mitchka*. Ya? *Mitchka* mean boiling, kind of... *mitchka*... kind of a privacy boiling. Simmer? Is that a privacy boiling? Simmer? But *mitchka* mean that she boil. What a great consequence, yeah? She is *mitchka* in the boiler room. I am tickle to myself on that.

Ah, you see, I am knowing your language! Before I come to Canada, I was translator. Ya? So, I am knowing your language, very details of your language. Example, think on this. In English the word *desire* is passive word. It's important word, ya? You want, you need, you love – but,

Kristen Thomson as DRACHMAN.

Photograph by Guntar Kravis.

you do nothing. Is something else that move you. But, in Bulgonian, that's my language, *udipine* is translate desire. *Udipine*: to lunge, to lurch, to seize upon, to fall like a bleeding monkey on all the bananas! *Udipine* is desire that have the will to possess. When your heart is full of *udipine* you are doing all sort of crazy thing. And that is the Bulgonian way and so, of course, I miss my country, ya? Bulgonia. "Mistress of the Black Sea. He caresses her shores, just above the knee." This is from our national poet, Ungar Bienheim. It is not possible to think on Bulgonia without thinking on Ungar Bienheim. He was carving that nation with his pen. He say: "We are white bears feeding. We are black bears hunting. Great Deer loping. Eagles swooping. Every jagged cliff is my home!"

I am not such an eagle in Canada, yeah? Except this bald head of mine. This hair of mine, I lost it when I was twenty-two. That was my first shit luck. I was actor at this time. It was like, it was like a signal from the theatre god – Drachman, don't act. Nobody want to see a bald leading man. Nobody wants to see bald twenty-two year old. Everybody want him off the stage immediately. So, I went from stagecraft acting to kind of translator, yeah? And then became dramaturge. Then, I was... ya...

He catches his reflection and points at it.

...finally that guy right there, he was Artistic Director National Theatre of Bulgonia. It's a comic. I was speaking in images to a mutilated nation and now I am, uh, sweeping your dust bunnies. But, that was my luck. That was my shit luck. And life is like that sometimes, isn't it? Life is sometimes... sometimes life is such a shit luck, it's hilarious. Don't you find that? And, as the famous Bulgonian axiom say: *Ich bat boekin ja wahlieh peitenieh.* The man who is always the same is a stranger to himself. It's a comic. I am used to work in the very best theatre, ya? Very highly-trained performers, very physical performers, very precise physical work. So what, what I'm doing here? Uh? What I'm doing here? Uh? I'm Custodian, ya? Kind of caretaker here at Greenfield Senior Elementary. So, now, ya, I am sweeping the floor, I'm polishing your knob, I am picking this vulgar juice box. But still, I have image and language for my blood and I have my red curtain. Practical the only thing what I was bringing with me from Bulgonia... because I was finding something so magical. I was finding after such a long years on the theatre that if you are simple putting red curtain, all sort of crazy thing have the possibility to happen. All sort of crazy thing.... Like this.

> *DRACHMAN turns on some teenage pop music and changes into CLAUDIA who is rocking out.*

Claudia

Some kids are mad when they're teenagers, right? Like in movies and at school lots of kids hate their dads. For different reasons at different times. Some kids hate their dad 'cause they want to shoot speed into their arms! Dads don't let them. Dads try to stop them. They say "Fuck off, Dad. Fuck off! I'm shooting speed into my arm and you can't stop me!" And that's 'cause they're into speed.

But I would *never* do that 'cause I don't hate my dad. My dad is my best friend and I get to see him every week! It starts Monday after school at 3:45. I wait for him in the park across the street from the school and he is never late like other kids' parents and we do something totally bohemian together like go bowling or for pizza. And I have to say, it is the best moment of my entire life because there's so much to talk about and we're both hi-larious. Like every time I say, "I'm thirsty," he says, "I'm Friday," which is just something between us, like father-daughter. And then we go to his apartment which is a downtown condo where I have my own room with a name plate on the door that says "Albert" for a joke and so

I say to him, I say, "al-BERT" – and I have lots of posters, no
pets, and I do homework and we just hang out and then I go
to sleep. And when I wake up on Tuesday morning it is the
worst day of my entire life because it's the beginning of the
whole next week of not seeing him. So I come down here on
Tuesday morning before class to get control of myself.

But Tuesday is also sophisticated because my dad
leaves for work before me so I get about twenty minutes in
the apartment all by myself, which is a very special time for
me which I think of as my teen time. Like, I drink juice but
I drink it out of a coffee mug. I look out over the vast
cityscape and listen to the top music of my time and, um,
okay. Mostly, I do my thing that I do. I take one of my dad's
socks from a pair and pack a snack in it, like a juice box,
pudding cup, whatever. I just do it for a joke-game to see if
he notices that something is missing.... And then I put hair
from my mother's brush under my dad's pillow to help them
get along. I learned that in voodoo class. And then I... um...
well... kind of, um... sneak around to find out information.
And there is a lot of information. Look what I found for
example six months ago! These! *(high heels)* I went to my dad
next time like, "look what I found by accident. What's? Like
whose are these?" And he goes like, fake normal, "Oh those
belong to Leslie."

I'm like "WHO?"

"Leslie is a special friend of mine."

Now, I don't want to sound precocious, but I know
a euphemism when I hear one. And then, when I finally saw
her I KNEW from her boobs how special she was. They were
like two flying saucers from another planet that came down
and landed on her chest! She came walking into my dad's
apartment on a MONDAY night all globbed over in nail
polish and lipstick and perfume AND wearing a mink coat

Kristen Thomson as CLAUDIA.

Photograph by Guntar Kravis.

with no care for the animals and high heels six feet off the ground! Which are bondage! They are bondage for women! You can get very, you can get very good supportive shoes. My grandmother died from osteoporosis and the bones in her feet like crumbled, they fell apart, and they had big knobs on them so she couldn't even hardly walk and she told me that it was from wearing high heels. So, I'm only twelve-and-three quarters and I already know that. And so Leslie is not very... um... not very... Leslie is... like... stupid.... She says, "Kiddo." She says, "let's you and me be such good friends, and just do girl stuff together, stuff your dad can't do 'cause he's a guy, and we can be such good girlfriends and you can tell me all your problems..."

And I'm like, "Think about it Leslie."

Like, that's just one example of her brain.

I find all my information from sneaking – all the important information about my own life, I find it from sneaking around. Like, I already knew my parents were getting separated from hearing my neighbours through the fence even though they didn't do it until my grandma died. And I already know that my grandpa's giving me my grandma's cameo for my thirteenth birthday. And... I know something else, bonecrushingly agonizing.

Okay. Here's what happened. Stacey and Tracey stopped talking to me again. We were doing our science fair project on rust – just pouring bleach on steel wool and observing it. But then they started ignoring me and passing notes. I was making the pie chart but now they can just shove it. So, then, I wanted to be partners with my best friend, Jojo. She is making a dinosaur out of chicken bones. Her father is an alcoholic on weekends, so she stays with her grandparents on Saturday night. They save the chicken bones and dry them out for her. But Jojo is in a different class, so I wasn't allowed to be partners with her.

And by the way, speaking of alcohol...

She produces a small flask of alcohol that
DRACHMAN has sipped from earlier.

Booze. I'm not going to say anything but he could get
so fired for that!

So, anyways, you know I have two goldfish, right?

She brings out her goldfish.

Romeo and Juliet and Romeo is pregnant! So,
I thought I would have an experiment of observing the
new family since I heard that goldfish eat their babies.
I didn't even know if that was true, so I went to my mom's
office to use the computer but she was on the phone so
I eavesdropped. Is that the right word? I listened. I heard
her say like " blah blah blah... David's getting married and
moving to Brantford. Blah blah blah..."

I'm like WHAT? I didn't even know if that was true.
So this morning, at my dad's, I'm just sitting there eating Fruit
Loops which I am too old to eat, and when he's just about to
go I go, "Congratulations!" He has a cardiac attack. Says he
wanted to tell me himself. So I felt really bad about that. Said
Leslie wants me for the flower girl. Said Leslie is honoured for
me to be the flower girl.

(to goldfish) I bet you never saw a flower girl before.
Flower girls never get to say anything. They just have to stand
there. They are usually five which is probably old in fish life
but it is young in human life. They don't get a statue on the
cake. They dress you up like they don't want you to look cool.
They *want* you to look like a loser.

You're not supposed to tap on the fish bowl 'cause it causes a sonic boom for the fish. I was going to take the fish up to class like "Yeah, you have rust, well, I have fish" but then I thought Stacey and Tracey might pour bleach in the water so now I'm keeping them down here where it's safe. So now my topic is like to observe "The Effects of Darkness and Greasiness on Goldfish."

Observation one. Spoke to the fish, no response. Conclusion. They don't speak English. Observation two. Fish grazed the side of the bowl. Conclusion. Swimming in circles.

You know what? If I was a real scientist, I would, I would slap the side of the bowl to discover what the sonic boom really does.

> *CLAUDIA changes into DOUGLAS in silhouette behind the red curtain. He emerges as if looking out the window of his apartment in the early morning.*

Douglas

I can hear those few wee birds just behind the traffic. Lovely. They've been keeping me sane since I moved up here. Big change to move up here. Very big change. I haven't lived alone since my wife passed, Eileen, so I moved up here about a week ago, maybe a few weeks. Yeah. That's right, I moved up here three months ago to be near my son – that's what I was thinking I wanted to say. That's why I moved. To be closer to my son David, my granddaughter Claudia, and his beautiful wife Cynthia. She's a custom-made lady! When those two met, they were so young, it was just like Romeo and Juliet – and now it's all gone to hell. That's right, and now he's mixed up with this new girl, this so-and-so. What's her name? Aw, Jesus Christ, what in the hell is her name? Now, I share

Kristen Thomson as DOUGLAS.
Photograph by Guntar Kravis.

my birthday with Jesus Christ, so I figure that gives me
a pretty good reputation. So for his sake and mine I wish
to hell I could remember the name of that girl. Audrey?

He begins the long process of unwrapping a candy,
speaking throughout.

Got a weakness for suck candies. Always have. Sweet
tooth. That's me. Sweet tooth, sweet toes, sweet heart. My
wife, Eileen always said a different part of my body. "Douglas,
you've got sweet knuckles." That's from knuckling around in
the candy dish, my darling. I have never seen a wrapper so in
love with a lozenge. Come loose, you devil. Eureka! We have
contact.

So, my son David's coming over with Claudia and
that new girl, whatsername? I'm meeting her parents. More
in-laws. Told Claudia I'd be her date to the wedding.
Meanwhile there's a nice lady down the hall, I was hoping to
take her. In any case, I'm going with old Hickory Dickory –
that's Claudia. Old Hickory Dickory Dock! That's what I call
her. She did the cutest little tap routine when she was... let's
see now... five or six years old. There was barely a tap in it.
Hickory Dickory Dock, tap, tap – that was it. The mouse ran
up the... you know, and then she'd spin around like she was
running up the clock. She puts up a fuss, but she'll still do it
if I razz her. In any case, they're coming to pick me up at six
o'clock. That's about eleven hours away. Got to get an early
start. Arthritis. Pain. That's what I say now when people ask,
I say, "Don't mind me, I'm just one big pain!" I think Eileen
would agree with that, wouldn't you dear?

"Douglas!" That's what she'd holler at me. Endlessly.
"Douglas!" But, when she was in hospital, she started calling
me Tom. She watched out the window of her room and said
she saw fish swimming out there in the parking lot. "Did you
feed the fishies, Tommy?" That was her baby brother. Very

confused. Very confused. But then right at the end there, she did, she looked right in my eyes, said: "Douglas, who was that pretty girl, Audrey?" Just like it was yesterday. But I never would have remembered that girl's name, not in a million years. Jesus Christ. All those years ago Eileen just showed up at the office. She just came walking into the office with the baby – and I was, I was, I was – mixed up with that girl. But she never said anything about it. She never. Not in all those years... until it was just near the end. I was touching her hair. She didn't have much left. Like a nest of feathers. She looked at me right in the eyes and said "Douglas, who was that pretty girl, Audrey?" I don't know who she was. I don't know. It's better to forget that... that...

That's what I wanted to say. They say that the first sign of going crazy is talking to yourself. Well, not in my case. In my case, it's about the fourth or fifth sign in my case. You hear those stories once you get to a certain age that you accept it and you want to move on? Well, nevertheless, I don't especially want to. I'd like to uh, I'd like to take another spin around the block. I really would. Which puts a nasty thought in my head. You hear that scandal in the papers about the nursing homes where the older people are living? They don't have enough staff, of course, goddamn places never do, and when they're getting too busy they're tying the old people up in the beds. Well, I thought, myself, I wouldn't mind being tied up by a few nurses. That doesn't sound half bad to me. Heavens. I say nonsense like that. You stop me. You stop me before I get started! Because that's the kind of nonsense, I'll say it though. I will. I'll say it.

> *DRACHMAN appears from behind the curtains and re-opens them. Takes the suck candy from his mouth: "I'm not so crazy on that suck candy;" picks up a juice box from the floor: "More Mitchka;" approaches his music source and before pressing play on some dance music says "This is going to be fun."*

Changes into LESLIE using the high heels that CLAUDIA showed us.

Leslie

Come on! Come ON! Pick it up! Pick it up! What's that name tag say? David? Leslie! Come on, you can do better than that, David! Hustle, baby, hustle! You are dancing with the creator of the Regional Supply Network! I don't want to brag but did you come to my seminar? I'm kidding. I'm kidding. I just want to party! I just want to have a helluva good time! That's why they hate me. That's why Michael's over there staring into his dink... I mean his drink!

When I started with the company Michael was my boss. He taught me everything about the company. He put in a lot of extra time with me *and* it's possible that there was a certain amount of... attraction on his part. I can hardly deny that. But, I'll tell you, he's a Christian and so I never thought it would end up in anything. I mean, I went over to his place for dinner a lot with his wife, Peggy, they've got three, Patty, they've got three lovely kids. They were very, you could tell that they'd been to church, "please" and "thank you" every-thing. After dinner, Michael would take me through every detail of the company's acquisition and distribution systems, which is where the RSN was born, really. RSN? Regional Supply Network. That's the system I developed! Come on, David, get with the program. Anyway, some nights we'd just sit in the kitchen and I'd spend the whole time just chatting with Peggy... I mean Patty. I was always calling Patty Peggy. I thought she was just going to take my head off.

What? What? Here I am going on about myself. Enough about me, what do you think of me, David? I'm kidding.

Kristen Thomson as LESLIE.

Photograph by Guntar Kravis.

Meanwhile, I am dating every conceivable version of Mr. Wrong. I was dating this one guy, so good looking, and he was pretty nice, treated me quite well. And uh, and then he just started acting like a maniac. He drove this big gold jeep. He used to come and park it out front of my building, all night long. Finally I did, I had to call the police – who did nothing. Until I spray-painted *Stalker* on his jeep. Told him if I ever saw his effing jeep again anywhere, I would do the same.

ALL OF WHICH, you see, brought out this over-protective thing in Michael because that's when he started dropping by my apartment. Then the gifts and the notes started. I told him, you know Michael, well, just look at him over there – I said to him, "Michael, you're fantastic, you're the best, you have been so good to me, but you're more like a father or an uncle to me than a" ...yeah. Then he went away. Yeah. After I told him that. I mean he went to Florida. And do you know what I think? I think he went down there and had a few affairs because that's when Peggy Patty left him. And he blames me for that. Oh yeah! He blames me for her leaving and she blames me for him having the affair! Oh yeah! Welcome to my world, David. That's par for the course. I'm used to it. Everybody! Got a problem? No, I'm serious. Any problems? Blame Leslie! Go for it! Do you have gas? It's probably my fault. Tell me, David, do you ever feel inadequate? 'Cause if you do, you can call me names 'til you feel better.

I don't know why I just said that. I'm kidding. I'm kidding. That doesn't actually happen. But seriously, seriously, it is, it is, it is challenging to be the only woman manager in that office – which is why I am so thrilled, don't tell anybody, I mean, who would you tell, but don't tell anybody. I've been offered a head office posting! Yeah. Brantford. Brampton? Did I say Brantford or Brampton? I always get those two mixed up. It's either Brantford or Brampton. It's Brampton. No, no, it's... where the hell is Brantford, anyway? Do you want to dance?

LESLIE dances into CLAUDIA, leaving her high heels in the space.

Claudia

I'm growing my hair out for my school photos. You know those school photo packages? I'm getting the one with me. Two blow-ups, one for my mom and one for my dad, and then two smaller ones and then six wallet-size photos. One for my mom, one for my dad, one for Jojo, one for Grandpa, one for Leslie, can you believe it? My dad said I have to give her my wallet-size photo and I have to put on the back of it like "LOVE Claudia." Anyway, it's going in my eyes so I've been getting eye infections. Yeah. Like, the grease on the end of my hair goes in my eyes and it makes my eyes get infected. But, right now they're fine. I can see you perfect. Yeah. I think my hair looks pretty good.

Some girls aren't even wearing their uniforms for their picture. Stacey told everybody that she's wearing hot pants and make-up. I might wear bell bottoms and platforms, but not hot pants. I think that they're just too short and my legs would just stick out of them so probably I wouldn't want my legs sticking out like that. Probably not. Especially for the home-room photo where it's not just your face but your whole body plus the whole class plus the home-room teacher, Mrs. Pritchard.

I like Mrs. Pritchard. She's hi-larious. She's so fat, she's sooo funny! She just is laughing all the time. Yeah. She teaches English. She gave us an assignment last week. So hard for the imagination. She said "Use a metaphor to express something about yourself." Like, that's pretty hard, right? Use a metaphor! That's just, like for one thing, I do feel a bit shy about using metaphors and also when you're an official pre-teen like I am, it's considered totally, like, pathetic to express anything about yourself. You're just supposed to act like, duh. Attitude, right? Like, what's an example? Okay. If an old-fashioned type of adult is trying to make friends with you they go, "Oh, what do you want to be when you grow up?" Right? And you should go, you go like this. "I don't know" just shrugging your shoulders, and like all over your face is like, duh. Right? But really the whole time underneath I know I wanna be a DJ or a VJ, 'cause that would rock! That would so rock my universe! Except it might be considered a bit pathetic. Because, like if I said it people might say, like, "How can you be a VJ? You're too ugly." Yeah. That's what people might say to me. But like if I said it I would have to be really cool to be able to say it. So I was just pretending when I said I wanted to be a VJ.

So anyway I tried to write a poem for my assignment, 'cause I like to write poetry. My dad said it's 'cause I'm sensitive. He said it's 'cause I'm sensitive and my mom said it's 'cause I'm emotional. But I couldn't finish it. I wanted to write about butterflies for my own personal reasons and how they start off as basically maggots and then go in a cocoon and then become a miracle but I could only write the first line, like:

You glide, you are throttled through
the black tunnel coming as
a shadow amongst shadows
with urges for light.

But, uh, I got writers block for the rest of that poem. So then I remembered an old dream poem that I wrote before I got my fish, dreaming that I had a sister. Yeah, an older sister. Like a sister who was like a rainbow with many different colours and many different moods and like arching over me to protect me. Just from anything. Just from grey skies. Yeah. But I lost it. Too bad, 'cause that was a very favourite poem of mine. So I had to hand in something, so

I handed in one that doesn't make any sense that was very um, unfortunately, that was very uh that was very ugly that's a very ugly nightmarish image called "Black Serpent" with the black serpent that lived in my stomach. And that sometimes got caught in my throat. And I would choke on it and in my poem I would choke on the black serpent but I could never get it out and I would be choking on the black serpent trying to push it out of my stomach, but it would always scoot back down in and lie there just coiled and ready to pounce at the bottom of my stomach. So, I got an A+, higher than Stacey or Tracey. Tracey compared herself to a horse for running cross-country. Duh. But I never showed that poem to my mom and dad even though I got the top grade. No. 'Cause if I showed them, sometimes if I told them that I'm upset or that I am um nightmarish or that I'm choking or that I just feel like sometimes if I said like "uh I'M NOT SO HAPPY AS I PRETEND TO BE!" I think that they would be pretty upset by that. If I just "IT'S A BIG CHARADE" I think that would really upset them. If I said "YOU SHOULDN'T'VE GOT DIVORCED" I think that that would really upset them a lot. And I don't want to 'cause, like, I always pretend that my mom's just fine, but, I HEARD HER CRYING. And she's, she's you know we do stuff together but she's not... sometimes I just watch her through the crack in the door. Sometimes I go in and I say "Oh are you okay? Do you want, um, some juice or like a foot massage or anything?" All the curtains are closed even if it's sunny outside. So, my mom is very sensitive. She is way more sensitive than me even though she's my mom. And my mom is way nicer than anybody else in the world. My mom is smart. My mom is brilliant. My mom is beautiful. And she is way better than anybody else, you know.

So, Leslie is not better than my mom. She is like she is like the crap on the bottom of my mother's shoes. Now, I have to say something nice about her, I know I do. Just a second. What do I like about her?

CLAUDIA puts on LESLIE's high heels and checks out her reflection.

Um... uh... I guess I feel kind of sorry for her in a way because I hate her so much because... I was looking through my dad's wallet and there was just one picture of Leslie in there. Like, the other picture was me and my mom so he couldn't keep that but... I still think he should have my picture in his wallet. But, I can't... "YOU SHOULD HAVE MY PICTURE IN YOUR WALLET." Like I could find another way to say it. A nice way to say it. Plus it's not a good time for causing problems. So, so, I just... I just one day, I just... I just said "oh that's a nice picture. Do you have any other ones?" So that's a different way of saying it – plus I'm getting my pictures done.

CLAUDIA becomes LESLIE in a bridal shop..

Leslie

Hello? Hello? Anyone? How much longer is this going to be? What am I, some kind of second-class citizen? Well, I'm not. And what bothers me, and I don't think I'm acting out of turn here, what bothers me is that I told them I have to get back to work. The dressmaker just turned around and stared at me with a mouthful of pins. He was working on some other girl who arrived at exactly the same time as me. I don't know why they double-booked our fittings, but she has got, I saw her dress, and I don't like it. It has got those big puffy, I don't even know what you call them, those big puffy...

(cell phone) Hello... don't worry, the dressmaker's not here yet. What's up? It'll be gorgeous. Did David call? Oh. Michael? Oban? What did he want? Did you tell him I was out of the office? Oh, he can't, can he. What's urgent?

He's known about that for two months. At you? What's his number – nine, eight? Five, eight? Thanks.

Admiring her new wedding shoes.

Aren't they sweet?

(cell phone) Michael Oban, please. Michael, don't yell at my secretary... don't yell at my sec.... Don't. No, I'm not talking to you until you agree not to bully my.... Yeah, bully. Bully, yeah... well, keep in mind that yelling is just a LOUDER VOICE and I can – not until you agree... all right. Oh Michael, you see that's not your department anymore, that's my department.... He doesn't have the trucks or the staff to handle the contra... yeah, 'cause he's your buddy.... It's not my job to keep him in business.... That's not bottom-line think-ing... as far as I can tell it's you who can't stop thinking about bottoms, just ask Pegpatty! ...Look, you've known about this for months... I already signed *Flatfoot*.... You know I mean *Fleetfoot*.... Well, you also probably think I shouldn't hang up on you right now but apparently I'm such a thoughtless bitch, I think I will... and anyway I'm at a fitting for my wedding dress right now. *(hangs up)*

They think they can just whip it together. Well, it's my wedding dress. It's not, uh, it's my wedding dress, it's not, it's not like uh some small thing. But nothing special can ever happen to Leslie.... That other girl arrived with her mother.

My mother, the only thing she's really focused on is that she wants an organ to play "The Wedding March". But I don't want a traditional wedding in the sense of a traditional wedding. But, that's what she wants. She wants a great whining organ groaning out "The Wedding March". So, I said to David I said, "Well, David, you know, maybe it's not such a bad idea 'cause you know what they say is even more

romantic than roses on a piano? Tulips on an organ!" He
had to agree with me there!

I love this pearly detail. It's so... just sweet.

Anyway, David doesn't really mind. It's not such a
huge thing on David's side. Not that he doesn't care, but with
the divorce... so it'll just be Claudia, his father, and a couple of
friends on his side. But on my side it will be a huge wedding
because, well, it's my first marriage and, oh God, well, I have
a bit of a reputation and it probably sounds stupid but I want,
I want, I just want everyone I know to see me walk down the
aisle with the man I love. That's what I want. And I really
want my parents to see that. I want it to be a perfect day and
I want to walk down the aisle right past them and give them
a little, you know, "fuck you." Like, you didn't think I could do
it, well, I did it. Kinda where I'm coming from. I know it was
the great joy of your lives to make me feel like an idiot, make
Leslie feel like an idiot, the greatest joy of your lives.... Pretty
grim, eh?

She puts on a wedding veil.

But somewhere along the line, maybe watching my
parents, I don't know, something snapped in my head and
went I'm not going to be miserable. I'm not going to be that
miserable. I don't wanna be. I just can't be that miserable.
And when I met him David was. He was. That's just a sad
fact. He just was a totally different guy. He was stiff, arrogant,
he had a terrible haircut... I still tease him about it. We were
at this conference and I was cutting loose on the dance floor,
I was kinda hammered, and I saw him standing there behind
his name-tag, handsome... but kind of incarcerated in his suit.
You know? Not at ease. So I just—innocently—grabbed his
hand and pulled him onto the dance floor and he started just
kind of tilting from side to side, you should have seen him.
Pathetic. Truly pathetic. But by the end of the night he was

covered in sweat, he had his suit jacket tied around his neck like a cape, I kept calling him Zorro, and his face was just beaming. So what are you gonna do? I met him at a time when he was feeling pretty depressed about his life and I know that feeling. I know that feeling very well. I had to take a little trip to the hospital once 'cause of that feeling. So... we just grabbed each other while the grabbing was good. And the grabbing was good. And I see him with Claudia and I think, I want you to be the father of my children too, 'cause I am nuts about her dad. Kookoo. What's the word I'm looking for? Bonkers? I'm kidding. I love him. 'Cause he's just washing all the pain away... just the regular pain. And when he looks at me, he sees someone worth loving. Now that's... that's a miracle.

> *LESLIE is wearing the veil and looking at her reflection. She enters into a fantasy about her wedding. She dances with DRACHMAN's magic top hat as if with DAVID, finally placing her veil and the top hat in a kind of wedding portrait. This image lingers as she changes into CLAUDIA.*

Claudia

Romeo and Juliet are dead. Juliet developed a big slimy growth, like infection on his eye. It was all long and white and trailing off his eye. And flowing around in the water. He looked like Leslie in her white wedding veil just trailing off her head like an infection 'cause they got married on Saturday. It wasn't even magical. And on Sunday the fish died. Juliet didn't even seem to notice the infection even though in such a small, cloudy fish bowl you think you would go mentally insane with such a big, long infection.

Too much fungus. That's what my mom said – from over-feeding. But feeding fish is practically the only thing you can do with them – especially to observe them scientifically. Otherwise they are just swimming. And what's swimming? It's not science! So, I kept sprinkling and sprinkling and sprinkling and sprinkling and sprinkling food in the water – until I became a murderess. And then guess what I found out fish food is made of? Crushed butterflies. Each little flake is a dried, crushed butterfly wing. So I'm writing one eulogy for everybody before flushing:

Fish to water, Wings to air.
Farewell to all that's gold and rare.

And when I'm finished I guess I'll just flush them.... And then yesterday, my science fair project was due. My class was supposed to set up our display tables in the gym but I just went home. I didn't even go to my dad's even though it was Monday 'cause he left on Sunday for his honeymoon in Italy. And today, it's Tuesday, so I wonder what's special about today? Armageddon? Just joking. I know what's special. It's a very special day.

Remember I said my grandpa was giving me my grandma's cameo for my thirteenth birthday? Well, what do you call this? That's my grandma when she was young. And who is wearing new platform shoes, even though my grandma wouldn't like it and even though my mom always swore no way, no way, no way, she would never buy me high shoes, high shoes are bad for growing feet but then she still bought me my dream shoes! Rock!

The shoes looks like a child's version of LESLIE's
shoes.

My dad gave me a million dollars to buy whatever I want. Just joking. He gave me two hundred dollars, though

– one hundred for graduating and one hundred for my birthday! And... the guy who's the janitor, he has the wizard face. He doesn't even have a very nice face. Some kids think he's scary but I don't. I saw him through a crack in the door. He pointed over there, said like "Ja, Jaaa" and closed the door behind him so quiet like a total librarian. Too bad he doesn't even speak very much English, we don't even speak the same language, except this note which I found: "Miss. A minor token for your commencement. Sincere Regards, Drachman, The Caretaker." And there was this.

The top hat. She looks inside and reads.

Made in Bulgonia. Weird, eh. I guess when you're a teenager, everybody can tell. When you're thirteen, even if you don't graduate into high school, still, you are, you are commencing on getting much needed guts and a subversive attitude towards the status quo.

Example. Science fair is going in the gym right now and I'm skipping 'cause I already know I'm going to fail. I already know that. So why should I pretend I learned something? And anyway that would be lying because I didn't learn anything. I just made a bunch of fake diagrams. Like this thing. This I did one day to show the pattern of the fish swimming in the bowl. What does it mean? I have no idea!

She tears the diagram.

So. Screw the science fair. So? Screw the wedding. Yup.

Stupid sucks, sucks so bad, that wedding sucked so bad. 'Cause I went to that wedding with my grandfather. I was just wearing sweat pants, I was just wearing crap pants to go and pick up my grandfather, 'cause I was supposed to get into my you-know-what dress. I had to go over to Leslie's with

her and all the bride maids and I had to spend time with her
and not with my even dad even though it was more a
special day of his and also it was practically my birthday-eve.
I hated that day so bad. And that's why it makes me so mad
and that's why I'm not going to talk anymore. And I already
told them that. I was mad like a teenager gets mad. On any
movies that I like now there's always a teenager that gets really
mad and goes into rebellion fits and I was like a total rebellion
fit. So you know what I did? Um, I had a public rebellion fit.
Because I was putting this dress – if you could have seen this
thing – on the back it had a big bow almost as big as my whole
bum, the whole bow. They even took a picture of me in it.
And then there was also, like, uh, a carousel flower circling
around my head. I took one look at myself–

And that's when I started screaming. I was! I was
screaming like a maniac.

"STOP THE PROCEEDINGS! I DEFY YOU
STARS! NOBODY ASKED MY PERMISSION!"

Can you imagine such pureness in front of everybody?
Staring at the congregation, shaking in my boots, knowing
I wrecked everything. Wrecked it! Wrecked it! Wrecked it!
Wrecked it! Wrecked it! Wrecked it! Wrecked it! Wrecked it!
Wrecked it! Wrecked it!

Standing there with a needle in my hand "WHO'S
GONNA BE THE WISE GUY WHO ASKS MY
PERMISSION OR I'M GONNA SHOOT SPEED INTO
MY ARM AND THEN I'M GONNA SNORT," like what
do you do with crack cocaine? "DO SOMETHING WITH
CRACK COCAINE TO MAKE ME ADDICTED FOR
LIFE AAAAND IF I'M SO ADDICTED I MIGHT END
UP, I might end up killing myself."

Kristen Thomson as CLAUDIA.

Photograph by Guntar Kravis.

The groom comes under a cardiac attack. Very serious.
Drags me back to the vespers, like the quiet church place,
whispering but screaming: "Why you little brat. How could
you ruin this day?"

And then I go like, "Ooooh yea, well, how come you
ruined my life? Now you only want to see me one Monday and
now you want to move even further in a different city."

He's like, "Blah, blah, blah... Leslie lives in Brantford,
Leslie is my wife, I love Leslie, Leslie, Leslie, Leslie, blah, blah,
blah..."

"Oh, you precious you are in love and now you get to
do whatever only you want and I am the garbage kid that you
can throw away in the garbage can of life!"

He's says I'm old enough to understand. "YES! I am
old enough to understand. So why don't I? Whose fault is
that? Maybe yours 'cause of what I found out."

Don't tell my mom.

That this conference coffee mug that I stole from my
dad's apartment actually belongs to Leslie. I thought it was
my dad's because it's from a conference he goes to every year.
But Leslie told me that it was hers. She said she went to the
same conference as my dad. The date on this coffee mug is
1997. But my mom and dad didn't separate until Grandma
died in 1999. "So you didn't split up because you were
unhappy but because you were a little too happy with other
people at a conference in 1997 when we were still a family."

Silence. Silence on the vespers. Okay.

He says that life is very complicated and that sometimes people don't mean to but sometimes people fail each other.

I said, "Yeah, you did fail. So I need some time to figure things out so I need to wear my own outfits for a while and not be the flower girl."

And he said, he said, "You're right. You are not going to be the flower girl, you are going to be the best man. I have a tuxedo rented for you in the back. Go put it on and we'll walk down the aisle together, pal. My darling, my love."

I said: "Really? Do you really mean it?"

He said: "Yeah, I really, really mean it."

And I said: "Is there a top hat?"

And he said: "Yeah, there's a top hat."

And so I went and put on my tuxedo and my top hat and even though I can't dance I did a soft shoe routine at the reception. And everybody laughed. And even my mom was there, she was, laughing and totally amazed 'cause everybody thought I was just gonna do Hickory Dickory Dock, but I did Fred Astaire. "Singin' in the Rain."

That really happened, you know. In my mind, I didn't wear that dress. In my mind...

Like, it's not even so much, like sometimes, I don't even know why I think it's my fault. I don't even know why. Like, sometimes the only thing I could think of is that my dad thought I was just too ugly. Maybe that's why he left... but that doesn't make any sense... but maybe I'm a butterfly.

Maybe I'm just in my cocoon right now. Maybe nobody thought of that but maybe I am. And maybe I will get better so that they, so that my mom and dad think that if I was good enough they better stick together to be my parents, right, 'cause I'm a really good kid. Has to have their parents, right? There's, there's, there's...

> *Unable to continue speaking, CLAUDIA becomes DRACHMAN.*

Drachman

> *DRACHMAN mops the floor as he talks. At the end the floor should be like a glimmering pool, reflecting the set, the lights of the theatre, etc.*

To conclude, I would like to tell to you famous Bulgonian fable, very short story, that my mother was telling to me when I was crying and so I was telling to my son, and so of course this story I am loving it very much. Yeah, I have a son, twenty-two, he is live in United State – but we are not talking on that.

Once upon a time, in a land as close as your thoughts, a naughty little spragnome was climbing through the window of a tiny straw hut and peek into the cradle of a newborn baby and whisper to her sleeping parents this promise. "Weave this child a basket to contain all what her heart desires and when it is full, I will return to make her wise." Now, I must stop to tell you that in Bulgonia we know this spragnome very well. He is very tiny, like my thumb, particular type of gnome which seem to do one thing, but always he is doing something else. So, to continue. Next morning, the farmer is cutting the straw and his wife is weaving that basket and for many years that child she take her basket and she go in her life gathering, gathering, gathering everything that her little heart want. Until her basket is so full. And when it's so full she have to put it down. Now, it's too heavy. Even so much pleasure, ya, it's not possible to carry on like that endlessly. You know. So she put her basket and so she go and she have a little sleep, something, and when she wake up she come back to find that her basket was complete empty! How did this happen? Well, on this moment, after such a long years, that naughty little spragnome is appear to her. She point on that crazy midget yelling "Thief!" And she begin to search on him and searching on every place for her stolen possessions until she see that she cannot find not one thing, not one hope remaining. All is gone. And so, she collapse on her basket and begin weeping, "Now I have nothing left but my sadness." And so she cry and she keep to cry until practical flood of tears was filling her basket. And when her basket is complete full of tears that spragnome point. He say: "Now, you see, your basket is no longer empty. Now it have very much inside. *Lugaldya*. Look." And when she look she saw that her basket was become a deep pool... brimming with her experience and dancing on the surface of her tears... yes, very clearly she perceived it. Reflected on the surface of her grief she saw herself.

DRACHMAN closes the red curtain.

The end.

I, Claudia is Kristen's first play for which she received the Arts Toronto 2000 Protégé Honours Award for Performing Arts from Urjo Kareda; and the 2001 Dora Awards for Outstanding Performance and Outstanding New Play. Kristen received a degree in Drama from the University College Drama Program at the University of Toronto and completed the acting program at the National Theatre School of Canada.